Life + Soul
LIBRARY

Why don't we all live together anymore?

Big issues for little people after a family break-up

Written by **Dr. Emma Waddington** + **Dr. Christopher McCurry**

Illustrated by **Louis Thomas**

Frances Lincoln
Children's Books

Contents

3 .... How to use this book

4-7 .... Introduction

8-9 .... Why is Daddy not at home anymore?

10-11 .... Are you ever getting back together?

12-13 .... Do you still love each other?

14-15 .... Is it my fault?

16-17 .... If Daddy left you, will he leave me?

18-19 .... Where am I going to live?

20-21 .... Will I have to go to a different school?

22-23 .... What about the cat?

24-25 .... Why do I have to live with you?

26-27 .... Am I going to have a new Mommy?

28-29 .... Why can't I do that? Mom lets me.

30-31 .... Why are you always being mean about Daddy?

32 .... Further reading and resources

How to use this book

This book has been conceived for you to share with a child. Each spread is themed by topic and should be used as a discussion point to help you to talk through common issues in childhood.

STEP 1   Turn to the spread featuring the issue you wish to discuss with a child. ●

STEP 2   Before sitting down with the child, read the advice from the authors explaining some common causes of behavioral patterns, and some tips on how to tackle them. ●

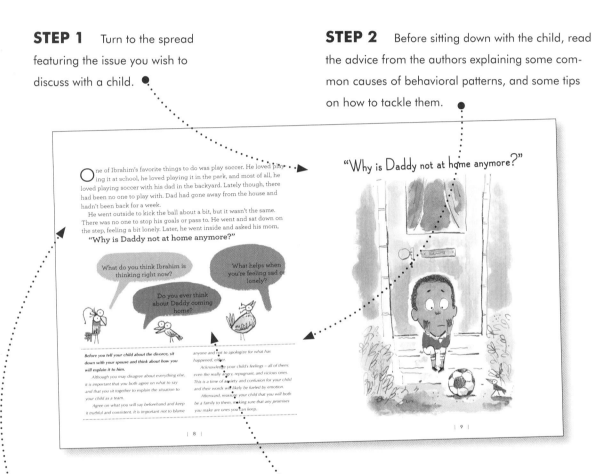

STEP 3   Direct the child's attention to the illustration and read the story that accompanies the scenario in front of them. This is a safe and non-confrontational way to approach a topic.

STEP 4   Explore the issue further with the conversational prompts that encourage the child to empathize with the scenario. This should ease you in to having a conversation with them about their own behavior.

Angus had been cross all day. Nothing was right, everything was wrong. At last, he asked, "Why is Daddy not at home anymore?"

How will this book help you talk to a child?

Divorce can be many things. It can be a time of heartbreak, confusion, and anger, filled with anxiety and doubt. Divorce may be a relief if the preceding months have been fraught with conflict and anguish. And for children, divorce can be all these things and more.

By its very nature, divorce is a time of great change. This can be bewildering and anxiety-provoking for children – and adults, too, for that matter. These changes invariably bring about a great number and variety of questions. Some can be answered simply and readily. Other questions require nuance and tact. And some questions, given the age of a child, simply can't be answered now. Some questions have no answer.

In this book, we aim to explain why a child may be asking these questions, and why questions are important in shaping a child's brain and their understanding of the

world. We will offer advice on how to respond (and why your answers matter!), and how to manage the emotions that may come with these discussions.

Certainly, with a topic as complex as divorce, we can't possibly address every potential situation and question that can come up. Nor can we, in this limited space, provide the kind of individualized and specific advice one might obtain from a counselor or psychologist. If you find you need more support in certain areas, turn to the back of the book where you will find more resources.

> Divorce is a time of great change that brings about all kinds of questions

How is a child's behavior connected to their developing brain?

Many questions from children are pretty mundane, but now and again they will ask something that leaves us dumbfounded, surprised, or, at times, hurt and upset, meaning that we cannot answer without further thought and time. This is certainly true when it comes to divorce.

Curiosity, however, is an essential ingredient for children's brain growth and development. As they explore and learn, children are building their brains – in particular, the front of their brains. This is the part that helps us make sense of our world. The front part of an adult's brain is huge, and this allows us to override the reactive back of the brain, in order to reason, slow down, evaluate, and make sense of situations and experiences.

However, up to the age of four, it is the back of a child's brain that dominates. This part of the brain (also known as our reptilian brain) informs us when something bad is happening and tells us to flee. This is a reactive part of the brain that was once essential for survival and is, by nature, very inflexible. This is why it can be so hard to calm a tantrum in full blast.

Unfortunately, the front and back of the brain are poorly connected, particularly in the very young. So when the part of the reptilian brain responsible for emotions like fear and anger (called the amygdala), fires up, it is very hard to tame.

As carers, we want our children to develop the front of their brains, as this will help them manage their behavior. This means that we can reason with them when they are in the midst of a fierce tantrum; we can ask them to wait, and they will, before jumping into the road, and so on.

So as children ask questions and hear your answers, these experiences are also shaping their brains – in particular, their frontal lobes. As they build these networks, our children will be better able to manage social situations, build stronger bonds, and act in ways that bring them joy and happiness.

When the part of the brain responsible for fear and anger fires up, it can be hard to tame

Why is what you say to a child important?

The answers you give to a child's questions shape their view of the world and of themselves. In this way, you are a child's first source of "truth" in the world, which influences their beliefs, concerns, views, values, and principles concerning how to behave – and will probably continue to affect their decisions for the rest of their life. No pressure!

But in all seriousness, nurturing a child and paying attention to the questions they ask will provide them with a point of reference or a compass that will help them to navigate their way through some of life's choppy waters.

What are some basic things to think about when children ask about divorce?

In times of upset and uncertainty, a child's question may be less about obtaining factual information (though that can be important) but instead be an attempt to convey some basic concern or emotion, such as anxiety or confusion. Questions become an opportunity for carers to convey understanding and acceptance, even if the child's distress seems unfounded, out of proportion, or is itself distressing for the adult.

Young children tend to see events in terms of how it will affect them in very immediate and concrete ways. Upon hearing that a well-liked teacher is leaving the school, a four- or five-year-old might ask, "Who will get us our snacks then?," whereas a seven-year-old might state that they will all miss Miss Emily. Similarly, questions about divorce may strike the parent as shortsighted and self-centered. That is to be expected among children.

A child may not have a strong initial response to being told of a divorce. It may take some time for the idea to become real or there may be a period of denial, of magical thinking that everything will suddenly go back to the way it was. Don't assume a child is doing just fine simply because she isn't talking about the divorce or asking what you might think are obvious questions. Periodic "check-ins," offering opportunities to talk and ask questions, while not insisting the child talk, can leave the door open for further conversation when the child is ready.

Answers to questions must, of course, be age-appropriate for the child. And, as a child grows and reaches new developmental phases, he obtains more sophisticated capacities for thinking about (and questioning) past events in new ways. This means questions can resurface years later as children grow. That may then be an opportunity to provide a little more information as appropriate, and to help the child develop a more sophisticated understanding of these events.

> Questions about divorce may strike the parent as short-sighted and self-centered

Why is good communication so important during times of stress and transition?

Ambiguity breeds anxiety. Be clear with your child and give out information as needed and when there is a clear, concrete plan; avoid speculation or half-formed ideas ("We might . . .") that could change or allow for conjecture on the part of the child.

When your child comes to you with a question, answer and then wait to see how they respond. Is there a follow-up? Does the child move on?

Most importantly avoid at all costs turning your child into a confidant during this difficult time. Similarly, try not to provide more information than is necessary (for example, things the ex has said or done, or financial matters), especially if you are doing this to gain support or validation from them. Cultivate and use your own adult resources.

Divorce will never be an easy experience for anyone involved, and during this time it is likely that your child will experience heightened emotions and ask more questions as they seek reassurance and security.

By finding ways to engage your child's curiosity, we will be activating their brains in different ways, giving them the tools to process and master their feelings.

By giving them reasons that are consistent with what matters to them in that moment, we will be helping them find meaning to their actions.

By making them feel understood and heard, we will be helping you manage the emotions that arise, and by being consistent in your expectations, you will be communicating the importance of these actions.

Together we will work on making you feel more confident in navigating the torrent of questions that we are faced with daily with commitment and care.

> Avoid speculation or half-formed ideas — ambiguity breeds anxiety

We look forward to working in this new way together!

One of Ibrahim's favorite things to do was play soccer. He loved playing it at school, he loved playing it in the park, and most of all, he loved playing soccer with his dad in the backyard. Lately though, there had been no one to play with. Dad had gone away from the house and hadn't been back for a week.

He went outside to kick the ball about a bit, but it wasn't the same. There was no one to stop his goals or pass to. He went and sat down on the step, feeling a bit lonely. Later, he went inside and asked his mom,

"Why is Daddy not at home anymore?"

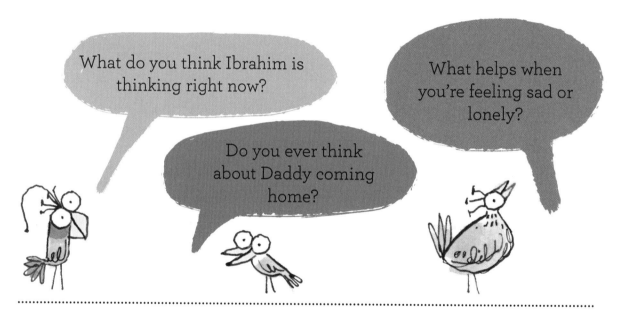

What do you think Ibrahim is thinking right now?

Do you ever think about Daddy coming home?

What helps when you're feeling sad or lonely?

Before you tell your child about the divorce, sit down with your spouse and think about how you will explain it to him.

Although you may disagree about everything else, it is important that you both agree on what to say and that you sit together to explain the situation to your child as a team.

Agree on what you will say beforehand and keep it truthful and consistent. It is important not to blame anyone and not to apologize for what has happened, either.

Acknowledge your child's feelings – all of them: even the really angry, repugnant, and vicious ones. This is a time of anxiety and confusion for your child and their words will likely be fueled by emotion.

Afterward, reassure your child that you will both be a family to them, making sure that any promises you make are ones you can keep.

"Why is Daddy not at home anymore?"

Angus had gone to stay with his grandparents. At the bottom of their garden was a hill. He decided to climb up it – it seemed a good place to have a think. The night before, his mom and dad had sat on either side of him and told him that they weren't going to live together anymore.

"Both of us still love you just the same," his mom had said.

"And we'll make sure we are always there for you, Angus," said his dad. But what did that really mean?

He climbed back down the hill, found his grandpa, and asked,

"Where am I going to live?"

Where is Angus going?

Do you ever wonder about where you're going to live?

What makes a house feel like a home?

Change is very scary for children. Suddenly being told their parents will no longer be living together will fill them with uncertainty. So wherever possible, keep the changes to a minimum. Keep them in the same home and the same room.

Your child will want to know the details of the new logistics. However, be careful not to overwhelm him with details. Be age-aware when you answer his questions. Younger children need fewer details. Also, keep the transitions and disruptions to a minimum. When it comes to visiting the parent who moved out, keep it simple. Don't interrupt your child's weekly routine. Keep the visits for the weekend. It also really helps if your child has a "transitional object" – something they can take and ferry between the two homes. This could be a stuffed toy, a car, or a book – whatever they love and makes them feel safe and cared for.

"Where am I going to live?"

Angus was on the phone with his dad. They hadn't seen each other for almost ten days, since his last weekend visit.

"Dad, can't you come back?" asked Angus.

"I'm sorry Angus, but your mom and I don't live together anymore. But I'll see you again this weekend. I've got something really special planned!" said his dad.

"But I want to see you now, not later!" said Angus. Then he added, **"Are you ever getting back together?"**

Do you think Angus is asking if his parents are going to get back together?

What answer do you think he wants to hear?

Do you wonder about this, too?

This question will linger in your child's mind, possibly forever. If you were together when your child was born, they will want it to be the same again.

We are surrounded by fairy tales and happy endings. This is what makes most sense to your child, so your child will want to believe that this is possible. For this reason it is really important to only tell your child about the divorce once it's one hundred per cent certain: no "maybes," no "perhaps." This way,

once the question arises on whether you will get back together, you can say "no." It is important that if the answer is "no," that you are truthful: uncertainty will be too overwhelming for your child, even if you wish it were possible to get back together. And while in the short term it would help them cope with the situation if they thought you would get back together, you must be honest. They will cope. You will be there to help them experience and manage their emotions.

"Are you ever getting back together?"

ngus was playing fetch with his dog, Rusty. It was raining outside, but that didn't matter, they could play inside the house instead!

They were up in his mom's bedroom when Angus threw the ball and it rolled under the bed. Rusty tried to get it, but his bottom wouldn't fit through the gap! Angus lay down on the floor to reach the ball, when he saw something else instead. He pulled it out, and saw it was a picture of his mom and dad, when they were still together. Just then his mom walked in and Angus asked,

"Do you still love each other?"

What do you think Angus is thinking when he looks at that picture of his mommy and daddy?

What can we do so you remember every day that we will always love you?

Do you ever wonder if we will ever stop loving you?

If parents can stop loving each other, then the fear is a parent can and may stop loving the child.

This is a natural deduction. Help your child with this fear by stating, as often as you can, that you love them. It might seem simple, but it will feel very comforting to them.

If the situation requires you to move out of the house that your child is living in, reassure them that you will continue to attend their important events – but be careful to be honest. Only commit to what you can keep to. Disappointments and let downs will come as a hard blow to your child, and increase any anxiety and confusion they may be feeling.

"Do you still love each other?"

O livia was in her room having some quiet time. She had been doing this more and more lately, since her mom had left the house.

It had been a few weeks since her mom had gone, and Olivia was trying to figure out what could have made her leave. Suddenly, she had a bad thought. What if it was because of all the times she had been naughty?

She called her dad into the room and asked,

"Is it my fault?"

Do you ever think you can't ever make a mistake or misbehave now?

Why does Olivia think it might be her fault that her parents are no longer together?

Do you ever think that?

"If I'd been a better child . . ." is a thought that can occur at any age. As adults and children alike, we seek coherence and look for the "reason" of events.

Young children are very simplistic. Their cognitive abilities are weaker and they seek to understand situations through cause and effect, such as "I hit my little brother: that is why Mom and Dad are fighting." It is natural that your child will think it could be their fault as they has been a part of picture at home. Your

child may even have heard arguments and noticed your unhappiness. It is important that you state very clearly that it is not their fault – even if they haven't asked the question. Similarly, they may ask, "Why did Mom leave us?" Explain that this was an adult's decision. If your child has heard your arguments, use that to explain what has happened: that as a family you will be happier with fewer arguments, yet you will still love each other very much.

"Is it my fault?"

Abby was at home packing her bags with her mom. Her dad now lived in another house and she was preparing to go visit him.

"Have you got your toothbrush and your teddy?" her mom asked her.

"Yes," replied Abby.

"Well then, I think you're all set to go see your dad," said Mom. But suddenly, Abby felt worried about the visit. Dad didn't want to see Mom anymore – so did that mean that he wouldn't want to see her, either? She asked her mom,

"If Daddy left you, will he leave me?"

What is Abby worried about?

Do you worry that we will leave you?

What can you do when you have that thought?

Children at a young age are very egocentric. Their world revolves around them.

As children get older, they start to see the perspective of others, but this only starts to kick in around age four, after which it takes a few years to properly operate. So, unless there were difficulties with separation anxiety, many children may never worry about parents "leaving them."

And yet, when divorce happens, this is a natural and logical deduction for a child to make. Help your child understand their experience by validating that this is a normal thought to have. Validate how scary it feels to think that Daddy could leave them. Reassure your child that this won't happen. Change is very scary, so explain how they will get to see Daddy: how often, when, and where. This will help your child start to understand the new situation and begin to come to terms with it.

"If Daddy left you, will he leave me?"

Ibrahim was at school but he wasn't feeling the same as usual. He was naughty in class and didn't even want to play soccer. His friends were worried about him.

"What's wrong with Ibrahim?" asked his friend Angus.

"His dad has gone away," said another friend.

"I'd hate it if my dad went away," they all agreed.

"Are you OK, Ibrahim?" asked his mom on the way home. "Is there something worrying you?" He answered,

"Will I have to go to a different school?"

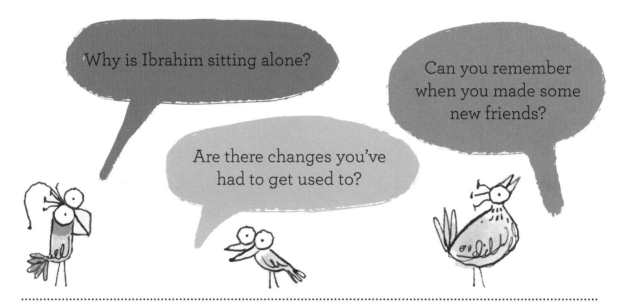

Why is Ibrahim sitting alone?

Are there changes you've had to get used to?

Can you remember when you made some new friends?

This question is asking for certainty. Predictability is so important to young children. They like to know where they will be.

When you explain to your child that you plan to divorce, they will probably keep asking you questions about where they will live, sleep, go to school, and anything else they can think of. The child is trying to make sense of the change that is happening around them. Be patient. Their brain is trying to accommodate this seismic change to their life.

Keep giving consistent answers and validating the emotion that lies behind your child's questions. In this case, they are probably feeling anxious. Ask them with curiosity, "Are you feeling worried about the changes that could happen?" This will create an opportunity for your child to tell you how they are feeling about it, and for you to reassure them.

"Will I have to go to a different school?"

Yuki was at home playing with her cat, Tama. Everyone in the house had been a bit cross and sad lately, but Tama would still purr noisily every time Yuki played with her, which made her happy.

Suddenly, Yuki had a thought. Her dad had moved out of the house, and they had told Yuki that she was going to stay at home with her mom, but they hadn't said what would happen to Tama. Who was she supposed to live with? So many things were changing so quickly! Her mom came into the room, and Yuki asked her,

"What about the cat?"

Why is Yuki worried about the cat?

Do you worry about your pets and other things?

What can we do to make it better for you and the pets when you're away from each other?

Young children think in very concrete ways and it is natural for them look to their immediate surroundings as they experience change.

Your child may not be able to anticipate future events. They will also struggle to deduce things due to their weaker cognitive abilities. Validate their emotions. They are probably anxious about what will happen to all the things that they love.

There will be a lot of fear and uncertainty for your child as the divorce proceeds. They may feel sadness and grief, and yet aren't aware of their emotions. Questions like these may be pointing to feelings of anxiety and sadness. Acknowledge that they may be experiencing these emotions. Help your child to label them. Answer these questions with short answers. Expect more questions to come. Over time, your child will start to get a clearer understanding and may not seek so much reassurance.

"What about the cat?"

Ibrahim's dad had come back to the house, but only for one evening. His mom and dad called him into the living room for a talk.

"Now, Ibrahim, you know that Daddy doesn't live at this house anymore," said his Mom.

"I will be living in a new place, just ten minutes away, so I won't be far," said Dad. "But it isn't very big, and there isn't a nice big backyard for you to play soccer in, like you have at this house. So we both agreed that it's better if you live with your mom."

This was a lot of news for Ibrahim to take in. He asked his mom,

"Why do I have to live with you?"

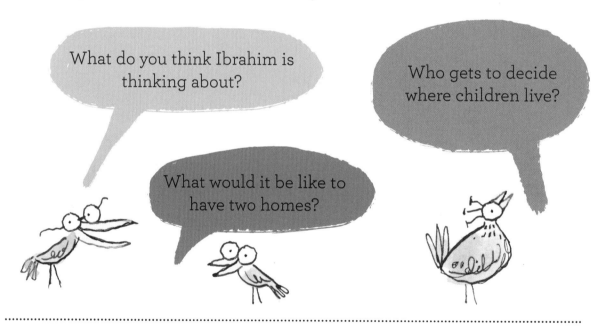

There are various reasons why your child could be asking you this question.

It could simply be out of curiosity: "How come I live with you and not Dad?"

Younger children will take longer to make sense of the new situation and will want to make sense of it all. Keep your answers short . . . And then wait for more questions.

Five- and six-year-olds may also have feelings of anger toward you. As they start to make sense of the situation, they may blame you for the divorce.

If there appears to be anger behind the question, acknowledge the emotion and validate that it's not an easy situation for anyone.

"Why do I have to live with you?"

BARIGHT PUBLIC LIBRARY
5555 S. 77th St.
Ralston, NE 68127

Angus was getting ready to visit his dad for the weekend. "I'm especially looking forward to this visit," his dad had said on the phone earlier that week. "I have a new friend – a lady – that I hope you'll like meeting!"

Who was this new friend? wondered Angus. What would they be like? Would Angus like them? And if he didn't, would that make his dad cross?

He started to feel a bit anxious, and called his mom into the room to ask her,

"Am I going to have a new Mommy?"

This is a question that is natural for a child to be curious about. They may be feeling anxious about the thought of having to accommodate another person. Or they may be an only child, so the thought of having stepsiblings could be exciting.

It is preferable to wait and leave a little time before you choose to start dating. Give your child sufficient time to adapt to the new situation before bringing in another person into your lives.

In the meantime, the answer to this question may be uncertain. Be honest. Allow your child to ask more questions about this. It is a novel situation, and scary, too, so validate the emotions that appear. Your child will be working hard to adjust to these new circumstances and will want to check out all the possible outcomes . . . including having a new parent.

"Am I going to have a new Mommy?"

I brahim had gone for the weekend to his dad's house.
"I know you like spaghetti and meatballs, Ibrahim, so I made your favorite!" said his dad.

"My favorite bit about spaghetti and meatballs . . ." said Ibrahim, putting the sieve on his head, "is playing space invaders!" And he jumped on the table.

"Ibrahim, get down at once! Where are your table manners?" asked his dad. But Ibrahim replied,

"Why can't I do that? Mom lets me."

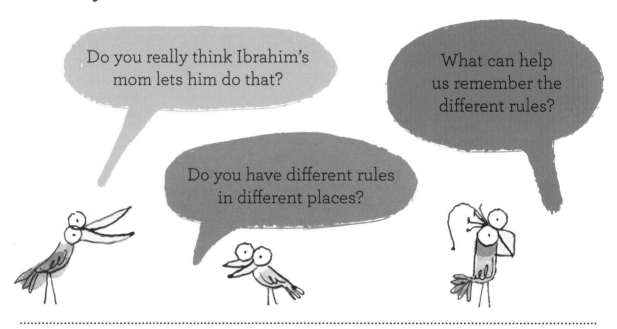

Do you really think Ibrahim's mom lets him do that?

What can help us remember the different rules?

Do you have different rules in different places?

Yikes! This is a difficult one – and yet very common.

Differences in parenting may have been part of the difficulties you faced as a couple, however, it is paramount that both of you share the same parenting priorities. You don't want your child to confuse the appropriateness of behaviors. Create a list of key behaviors and the rules. Stick to these. Accept that some behaviors may not be as important: how much

TV your child watches, for example, may vary, yet it's not as important as whether they can hit or spit. Here you need to be clear and consistent. In cases without clear-cut boundaries, clarify that the rules are different for certain things in each house. Validate that it is confusing. Acknowledge your child's wishes. And then set the boundary. If you are consistent, eventually your child will acclimatize to the differences in rules.

"Why can't I do that? Mom lets me."

Olivia had gone to visit her mom. "Well, it is a shame that you are late, but I guess I shouldn't be surprised. Your father was always late," said her mom. Then she went upstairs and told Olivia to come and unpack. But when she opened up Olivia's case, her mom got cross again. "Look at these clothes! Nothing is folded properly and it's all wrinkled and creased. I suppose he thinks I should still do all the ironing! And another thing—"

But Olivia didn't want to hear any more cross words from her mom, and asked,

"Why are you always being mean about Daddy?"

What do you think Olivia's mom is saying to her?

Is it ever OK to say mean things?

What are some ways we can talk about worries and problems without being mean?

This is a wake-up call! There are lots of reasons you may want to talk badly about your ex-partner. Being divorced will bring a lot of complex emotions and situations to deal with. However, these must not be seen by your child.

Put all your energy into being civil and caring with each other. Research shows that children suffer most when parents are fighting. Make sure you don't speak about your partner to anyone within earshot of your child, they will hear it. Don't ask your child to take sides – even subtly. It is natural to have many strong emotions of your own, but if you need support, seek another adult or therapist.

"Why are you always being mean about Daddy?"

Further reading and resources

Books to read with children

Brown, L., & Brown, M. *Dinosaurs Divorce* (New York: Little, Brown and Co., 1988)

Masurel, C. *Two Homes*. (Somerville, MA: Candlewick Press, 2003)

Books for parents

Long, N., & Forehand, R. L. *Making Divorce Easier On Your Child: 50 Effective Ways To Help Children Adjust* (New York: McGraw-Hill, 2002)

Wolf, A. E. *Why Did You Have To Get A Divorce? And When Can I Get A Hamster?* (New York: Farrar, Straus and Giroux, 1998)

Websites

aamft.org/imis15/AAMFT/Content/Consumer_Updates/ Children_and_Divorce.aspx. Advice from The American Association for Marriage and Family Therapy.

https://www.aacap.org/AACAP/Families_and_Youth/ Facts_for_Families/FFF-Guide/Children-and-Divorce-001. aspx, Advice from The American Academy of Child and Adolescent Psychiatry.

kidshealth.org/parent/positive/talk/help_child_divorce. html. From the Nemours Foundation, A parent's guide to talking to children about divorce and helping them cope.

webmd.com/parenting/features/top-5-mistakes-divorced- parents-make. http://www.webmd.com/parenting/kids- coping-divorce. Both from WebMD.

Why don't we all live together anymore? copyright © Frances Lincoln Limited 2016
Text copyright © Dr. Emma Waddington and Dr. Christopher McCurry 2016
Illustrations copyright © Louis Thomas 2016

First published in the USA in 2016 by Frances Lincoln Children's Books,
an imprint of Quarto Inc.,
276 Fifth Avenue, Suite 206, New York, NY 10001
QuartoKnows.com
Visit our blogs at QuartoKnows.com

All rights reserved

No part of this publication may be reproduced, stored in a retrieval system, or transmitted,
in any form, or by any means, electrical, mechanical, photocopying, recording or otherwise
without the prior written permission of the publisher.

Edited by Jenny Broom • Designed by Andrew Watson
Production by Laura Grandi
Published by Rachel Williams

ISBN: 978-1-84780-867-7

Printed in China

1 3 5 7 9 8 6 4 2

MIX
Paper from responsible sources
FSC
www.fsc.org
FSC® C104723